To my wife Barbara. To Sarah. To Daniel.

# my BEST

# PIERRE

# HERMÉ

ALAIN DUCASSE

PUBLISHING

# PIERRE HERMÉ

**Which pâtissiers have influenced you most?**

At the age of twelve, I knew that I wanted to be a pastry chef. Thanks to an advertisement that appeared in *Les Dernières Nouvelles d'Alsace*, I went to Gaston Lenôtre when I was fourteen to start my apprenticeship. Although I had already worked with my father, I had to start again from scratch! It was there that I learned attention to detail, and the importance of organization and precision. Even today, this is a landmark, a true foundation. Another pastry chef who has contributed a great deal to the development of this trade is Pascal Niau, the *grand chef pâtissier* at Dalloyau. In the early 1980s, I would stand in front of their display case asking myself how this or that that had been made—I was amazed. Yves Thuriès also made me dream, with his encyclopedia of pâtisserie, which influenced creative cuisine in the eighties.

**How do you create your pastries?**

I create tastes, associations of flavors; sometimes I reinterpret a well-known flavor, which I then associate with a product (cake, macaron, ice cream). In this way, Ispahan (to begin with, this was a blend of rose and raspberry, which I called Paradise, at Fauchon) is a cake made of rose macaron, rose cream, raspberries, and lychees. I then reworked it in a completely different way to create a jam, a fruit paste, a chocolate candy, a croissant, a cake, a sorbet… the blend is rethought, reinterpreted, every time.

I write and I draw sketches of my recipes, so as to make the confectioners who work with me understand how I imagined it when they taste it. Textures, sensations—I have them in my head, in the same way a musician would have notes. After that, we change the techniques, the way we make them. Then it's time to taste: During this, I alter certain elements if necessary.

**What role do the ingredients play?**

There are ten principal ingredients in pâtisserie: milk, butter, cream, eggs, sugar, flour, vanilla, chocolate, almonds, and fleur de sel—sea salt crystals. Salt is important in sweet cookery; that's what puts sugar on a pedestal! Chocolate occupies a separate place, since this is one of the gourmet's favorite tastes. It's an infinite ingredient, which I'm still learning about every day. I use pure, original chocolate from small farms in very specific regions so as to have interesting flavors—as in my work with Valrhona and François Pralus.

**How does your creativity show itself?**

Every recipe is capable of evolution. I don't have any taboos about this: If I can see a way of improving any cake, I let the recipe develop. So for the croissant or the *crème pâtissière*, the recipe is not fixed. Taste is a form of general growth, which enhances itself by sampling new ingredients. The capacity to create depends on the culture of taste.

| IN FIVE DATES | 1961 (November 20) | August 1976 | 1986 |
| --- | --- | --- | --- |
| | \| | \| | \| |
| | Born in Colmar | Started apprenticeship with Gaston Lenôtre | Head pastry cook at Fauchon, until 1996 |

You should never be satisfied with what you learn, but always try to learn more. Just like a student who is taking courses, doing exercises, and undertaking research, being proactive allows you to acquire knowledge and techniques by yourself, through reading, research, discussions with your peers.

**How should we use the recipes in this book?**
By making all the preparations, just like I do when I cook a savory recipe at home: Read the whole recipe carefully, plan out the steps, check the ingredients and the equipment… and the first time, follow the recipe exactly as it is written.

**What makes a great dessert?**
A great dessert manages to create different emotions with every mouthful.

# GOURMET **PORTRAIT**

**1/** WHAT IS THE TOOL YOU CAN'T MAKE PÂTISSERIE WITHOUT?
The pastry chef's trio: scales, thermometer, timer.

**2/** WHAT IS YOUR FAVORITE DRINK?
With cakes, Sencha green tea. Its delicate bitterness refreshes the palate after every mouthful. Wine tastes better after dessert.

**3/** WHAT IS THE COOK BOOK THAT MARKED YOU?
*Pralinés passe-partout*, a book that belonged to my father, where you find all the Swiss chocolate tradition. This tradition is the foundation of French know-how. This book inspired my father to make his creations. It was this book that taught me the history of chocolate-making.

**4/** WHAT ARE YOUR SECRET WEAKNESSES?
A good wine, a Krispy Kreme doughnut, a pastrami sandwich at Katz in New York, Kobe beef…

**5/** WHAT IS YOUR FAVOURITE DISH?
In winter, blanquette and pot-au-feu.
In summer, beef gravelax and ceviche.

**6/** IF YOU HADN'T BEEN A PASTRY CHEF, WHAT WOULD YOU HAVE LIKED TO BECOME?
When I was younger, I thought of maybe being a gardener or an architect. But in the end, I never wanted to be anything other than a pastry chef!

**7/** WHAT IS YOUR MOTTO?
I like attention to detail more than the pursuit of perfection.

# CON TENTS

ISPAHAN
08

2000 FEUILLES
16

CARRÉMENT CHOCOLAT
26

PLAISIRS SUCRÉS
34

TARTE FINE CHLOÉ
42

## TARTE INFINIMENT
### VANILLE
# 50

## ÉMOTION
### ENVIE
# 58

## SURPRISE
### CÉLESTE
# 66

## MISS GLA'GLA
### MONTEBELLO
# 76

## RÉVÉLATIONS
### (TOMATO/STRAWBERRY/OLIVE OIL)
# 84

## MACARON
### MOGADOR
# 92

# ISPAHAN

This cake is a subtle blend of rose petal cream, soft and smooth, with lychees, whose flavor enhances the rose and raspberry tastes with its contrasting acidity and power—all within a soft yet crunchy macaron envelope.

# RECIPE

**SERVES 6 TO 8 - Preparation time: 90 minutes - Cooking time: 60 minutes**

DRINK PAIRING:
*Gewurztraminer Grand Cru or Gewurztraminer Vendanges Tardives,*
*Gewurztraminer Sélection de Grains Nobles, Jardin de Pierre tea.*

**PINK MACARON**

- ❐ 8 ¾ oz (250 g) confectioners' sugar
- ❐ 8 ¾ oz (250 g) ground almonds
- ❐ A few drops crimson food coloring
- ❐ 6 egg whites (6 ¼ oz/180g)
- ❐ ¼ cup (65 ml) mineral water

- ❐ 8 ¾ oz (250 g) superfine sugar

**ITALIAN MERINGUE**

- ❐ ⅓ cup (75 ml) mineral water
- ❐ 8 ¾ oz (250 g) superfine sugar
- ❐ 4 egg whites (4 ¼ oz/120 g)

**ROSE PETAL CREAM**

- ❐ 3 to 4 egg yolks (2 ½ oz/70 g)
- ❐ 1 ½ oz (45 g) superfine sugar
- ❐ 6 tablespoons (90 ml) fresh whole milk
- ❐ 16 oz (450 g) soft butter at room temperature
- ❐ A few drops rose essence (from the drugstore)
- ❐ 1 oz (30 g) rose syrup (in Asian groceries

or under the brand name Monin)

**ASSEMBLY**

- ❐ 7 oz (200 g) lychees in syrup, drained
- ❐ 8 ¾ oz (250 g) fresh raspberries
- ❐ 5 red rose petals
- ❐ Glucose

10

## Pink Macaron

Sift* the confectioners sugar with the ground almonds. Mix the coloring with 3 egg whites. Pour this onto the sugar/almond mixture and mix. Boil water and sugar to 245°F (118°C). When the syrup reaches 230°F (110°C), begin to beat the other three egg whites to form soft peaks. Pour the syrup on the egg whites. Beat, and allow to cool to 120°F (50°C) before folding it into the sugar/almond/coloring mixture, allowing the beaten egg whites to settle.

**01**

Pour the mixture into a pastry bag with a plain No. 12 nozzle. Pipe spirals to make 8-inch (20-cm) diameter circles on a baking tray covered with a Silpat mat. Leave the circles to form a crust for at least 30 minutes at room temperature. Preheat the oven: convection oven at 350°F (180°C). Slide the tray into the oven. Bake for 20 to 25 minutes, quickly opening and shutting the oven door twice during cooking. Remove from oven, leave to cool.

**02**

*Keep refrigerated until ready to serve.*

* see glossary p. 100/101

## Italian Meringue

Bring the water and sugar to a boil in a saucepan. As soon as it boils, clean the edges of the saucepan with a damp pastry brush. Leave to cook to 245°F (118°C). Beat the egg whites to soft peaks (that is, not too firm). Pour the sugar syrup onto the beaten egg whites. Allow to cool while continuing to beat. You will use only 6 ¼ oz (175 g) of this meringue.

03

## Rose Petal Cream

Beat the egg yolks and sugar together. Boil the milk and pour it on to the egg-yolk sugar mixture. Cook like a custard to 180°F (85°C), then cool very quickly in the bowl of a stand mixer fitted with a beater. Be careful, as this mixture can easily stick to the bottom of the saucepan during cooking.

04

*It is best to use egg whites that have been kept for a few days at room temperature.*

In the bowl of a stand mixer, using first the blade and then the whisk, whip the butter until it is light and fluffy*. Add the cooled custard and mix. Incorporate the Italian meringue by hand, and add the rose essence and the syrup. Use immediately.

**05**

Cut the lychees into two or three pieces, depending on the size of the fruit, and leave to drain overnight in the refrigerator. Put the first pink macaron, upside down, on a dish. Using a pastry bag fitted with a No. 10 nozzle, pipe a spiral of cream in the shape of rose petals, arrange the raspberries in a ring around the outside edge of the macaron, so that they can be seen, then arrange two other rings of raspberries inside, following the shape of the macaron.

**06**

*You can keep this macaron in the refrigerator for two days.*

Arrange the lychees between the rings, pipe another rose-petal shaped spiral of cream over them, and lay the second pink macaron on top, pressing lightly.

Decorate the top with three fresh raspberries and five red rose petals, set off with a dewdrop made of glucose, which you can pipe on with a plastic or parchment-paper cone.

*Make the Ispahan the day before, so that it is soft.*

# 2000 FEUILLES

This praline millefeuille* combines a series of crunchy and soft textures with layers of Gavottes Crispy Lace Crepes, which give the praline its flaky texture.

# RECILE

DRINK PAIRING:
*Corsican Muscat, Vin Cuit from Provence.*

### ROASTED, BLANCHED ALMONDS AND HAZELNUTS

- 2 ½ oz (70 g) whole almonds
- ½ oz (20 g) whole Piedmont hazelnuts
- 8 ¾ oz (250 g) superfine sugar
- 2 ½ oz (75 ml) mineral water

### HAZELNUT PRALINE LEAVES

- 2 tsp (10 g) butter
- ½ oz (20 g) 40% cocoa Jivara Valhrona chocolate
- 1 ¾ oz (50 g) hazelnut praline 60/40
- 1 ¾ oz (50 g) pure hazelnut paste (hazelnut purée)

- 1 ¾ oz (50 g) crumbled Gavottes Crispy Lace Crepes
- ½ oz (20 g) roast hazelnuts, crushed

### INVERTED PUFF PASTRY

- 17 ½ oz (490 g) butter
- 1¼ lb (500 g) T45 flour
- ⅔ cup (150 ml) mineral water
- ½ oz (17 g) fleur de sel
- A few drops white vinegar

### CARAMELIZED PUFF PASTRY

- 1 ¾ oz (50 g) confectioners sugar

### CONFECTIONERS' CUSTARD

- 2 cups (500 ml) whole milk
- 1 oz (5 g) vanilla pod

- 5 ¼ oz (150 g) superfine sugar
- ½ oz (15 g) flour
- 1 ½ oz (45 g) Maïzena (cornstarch)
- 7 egg yolks (5 oz /140 g)
- 2 oz (60 g) unsalted butter

### ITALIAN MERINGUE

- ⅓ cup (75 ml) mineral water
- 8 ¾ oz (250 g) superfine sugar
- 4 egg whites (4 ½ oz/125 g)

### ENGLISH CUSTARD

- 7 egg yolks (5 oz/140 g)
- 3 oz (80 g) superfine sugar
- ¾ cup (180 ml) fresh whole milk

### BUTTERCREAM

- 13 ¼ oz (375 g) unsalted butter, at room temperature
- 6 ¼ oz (175 g) custard
- 6 ¼ oz (175 g) Italian meringue

### PRALINE BUTTERCREAM

- 8 ¾ oz (250 g) buttercream
- 1 ¾ oz (50 g) hazelnut praline 60/40
- 1½ oz (40 g) Fugar pure hazelnut paste

### PRALINE CHIFFON CREAM

- 2 oz (60 g) confectioners' custard
- 12 oz (340 g) praline buttercream
- ⅓ cup (70 ml) whipping cream, whipped

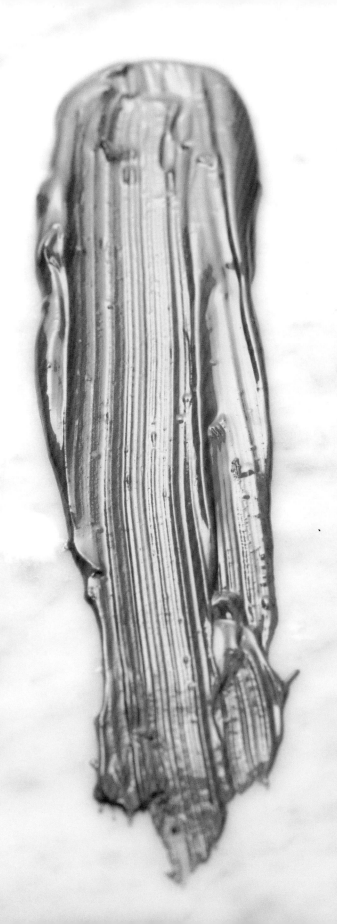

**Roasted, Blanched Almonds and Hazelnuts**

Spread the almonds on a baking sheet and place it in the oven for 20 minutes at 325°F (160°C). Set aside. Repeat with the hazelnuts, then crush hazelnuts.

Heat the sugar and water together to 245°F (118°C), then pour it over the almonds. Caramelize this over the heat. Pour the caramelized almonds on a baking sheet covered with a Silpat mat, then mix, while spreading them out to cool. Keep them in an airtight container.

**01**

**Hazelnut Praline Leaves**

Melt the butter and chocolate at 110°F (45°C) in a bain-marie*. Mix the hazelnut praline and the hazelnut paste into the melted chocolate and butter. Add the crumbled Gavottes and the roasted, crushed hazelnuts. Fill a 7-by-7 inch (17 by 17 cm) tin with 7 oz (200g) of hazelnut praline. Smooth the surface with an offset spatula and put the tins in the freezer.

**02**

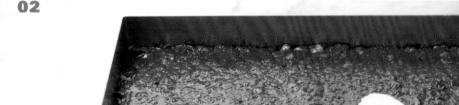

## Inverted Puff Pastry

Work 13 ¼ oz (375 g) of butter and 65 ¼ oz (150 g) of flour together so that they are completely blended. Roll into a flattened ball and wrap in plastic before putting it into the refrigerator for an hour. Loosen it by mixing in the other ingredients, shape into a square, wrap in plastic and leave to rest for an hour. Loosen it with the butter-flour mixture. Give two double turns at 2-hour intervals, leaving the pastry in the refrigerator between turns, then a single turn before rolling out.

**03**

Roll the puff pastry out to the dimensions of a baking tin (24 by 16 inches/60 by 40 cm) and prick it with a fork. Lay a sheet of parchment paper on the tin, then place the pastry on top. Slide the tin into the refrigerator: The dough must rest for at least two hours so that it rises properly in the oven and cooks without shrinking. You can store the pastry scraps in the freezer. Preheat the oven to 450°F (230°C). Sprinkle the pastry with 3 oz (80 g) of superfine sugar and put it in the oven while lowering the temperature to 375°F (190 °C).

**04**

## Caramelized Puff Pastry

Let the pastry cook for 10 minutes, then cover it with a broiling pan and continue cooking for 8 minutes. Take the pastry out of the oven, remove the broiler and turn the pastry over on to a sheet of parchment paper. Remove the paper from the underside and sprinkle it evenly with confectioners sugar before putting it back into the oven at 480°F (250°C) to finish cooking for a few minutes.

**05**

**Prepare the confectioners' custard.** Boil ½ cup (125 ml) milk with the vanilla pod and leave to infuse for 20 minutes. Strain this infusion through a muslin cloth. Add the rest of the milk with 1 ¾ oz (50 g) superfine sugar and boil. Sift the flour and Maïzena. Add the egg yolks and the rest of the sugar to this mixture. Blend this mixture into the milk, bring a boil, and leave to cook for 5 minutes while whipping, then pour into a bowl to cool. Add half of the butter, mix, then stir in the other half. Lay a sheet of plastic on the surface (to prevent a skin from forming) and store in an airtight container. **Italian Meringue.** Make an Italian meringue (see p. 102).

**06**

*The surface of this caramelized pastry is smooth and glossy while the underneath it is sweet and crunchy because of the layer of superfine sugar in the pastry at the start of cooking.*

**English Custard**

Make an English custard (see p. 102), and cool quickly in the bowl of a stand mixer fitted with a whisk. Be careful, as this mixture can easily stick to the bottom of the saucepan during cooking.

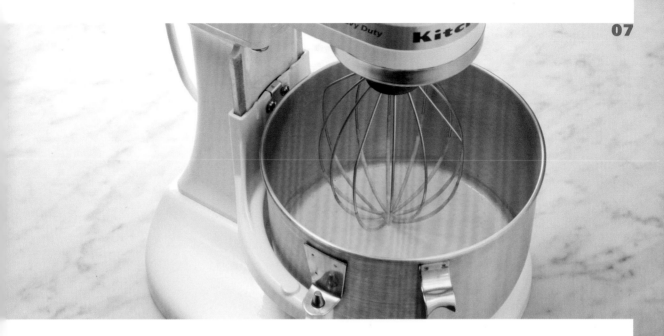

07

**Buttercream**

In the mixer, with a whisk, whip the butter until it is light and fluffy*. Add the English custard and mix before working in 6 ¼ oz (175 g) of Italian meringue, by hand. Use immediately.

08

## Praline Buttercream

In the mixer, whip 8 ¾ oz (250 g) buttercream until it is light and fluffy*, then add the praline and the hazelnut paste.

## Praline Chiffon Cream

In a bowl, soften the confectioners' custard with a whisk. In the mixer, whip 12 oz (340 g) praline buttercream until it is light and fluffy*, then add the confectioners' custard. Work in the whipped cream by hand. Use immediately.

**09**

**10**

## Assembly

Cut three squares of caramelized puff pastry, measuring 7-by-7 inches (17 by 17 cm).
Put a square of caramelized pastry on a baking sheet, glossy caramelized side up. Using a pastry bag without a nozzle, spread it with 3 ½ oz (100 g) of praline cream, lay on a frozen praline leaf, and decorate with another 3 ½ oz (100 g) of cream.

**11**

*Keep in the refrigerator until ready to ready to serve.*

Lay a second square of caramelized pastry on top, then, using a pastry bag, cover it uniformly with 8 ¾ oz (250 g) of cream and finish with a last square of caramelized puff pastry.

Powder the corners of the millefeuille of with confectioners sugar and decorate with a few roasted, caramelized almonds.

*The inverted puff pastry has the following advantages: It is crunchier and gooier, it shrinks less in cooking, and it keeps better when frozen.*

# CARRÉMENT
# CHOCOLAT

A cake entirely made of chocolate, dedicated to lovers of its intense bitterness: a play on textures and temperatures, between the soft, the smooth, and the crunchy.

# RECEIPE

SERVES 6 TO 8 - Preparation time: 90 minutes - Cooking time: 45 minutes

DRINK PAIRING:

*Rivesaltes Rancio Domaine du Vieux Puits, from David Moreno at Villeneuve de Corbières,*
*Maury Mas Amiel Vintage from Charles Dupuy.*

## MELTED CHOCOLATE BISCUIT

- ❒ 4 ½ oz (125 g) 70% cocoa Guanaja chocolate from Valrhona
- ❒ 4 ½ oz (125 g) softened butter
- ❒ 4 oz (110 g) superfine sugar
- ❒ 2 eggs (3 ½ oz/100 g)
- ❒ 1 ¼ oz (35 g) sifted flour*

## SILKY CHOCOLATE CREAM

- ❒ 3 egg yolks (2 oz/60 g)
- ❒ 2 oz (60 g) superfine sugar
- ❒ ½ cup (25 ml) fresh whole milk

- ❒ ½ cup (25 ml) heavy cream
- ❒ 3 ¼ oz (90 g) 70% cocoa Guanaja chocolate from Valrhona, finely chopped

## DARK CHOCOLATE PRALINE

- ❒ 2 teaspoons (10 g) unsalted butter
- ❒ 1 oz (20 g) Extra Valrhona cocoa paste (100% cocoa)
- ❒ 1 ½ oz (40 g) almond praline 40/60 (Valrhona)
- ❒ 1 ½ oz (40 g) pure hazelnut paste (hazelnut purée)
- ❒ 1 oz (25 g) crumbled Gavottes Crispy Lace Crepes

- ❒ 1 oz (20 g) cocoa nibs

## CHOCOLATE MOUSSE

- ❒ 6 oz (170 g) 70% cocoa Guanaja chocolate from Valrhona
- ❒ ⅓ cup (80 ml) fresh milk
- ❒ 1 egg yolk (½ oz/20 g)
- ❒ 4 egg whites (4 ¼ oz/120 g)
- ❒ 1 oz (20 g) superfine sugar

## CHOCOLATE SAUCE

- ❒ 4 ¾ oz (130 g) 70% cocoa Guanaja chocolate from Valrhona
- ❒ 1 cup (250 ml) mineral water

- ❒ 3 ¼ oz (90 g) superfine sugar
- ❒ 4 ½ oz (125 g) heavy cream

## CHOCOLATE ICING

- ❒ 3 ½ oz (100 g) 70% cocoa Guanaja chocolate from Valrhona
- ❒ ⅓ cup (80 ml) heavy cream
- ❒ 1 oz (20 g) unsalted butter

## THIN SHEET OF CRISPY CHOCOLATE

- ❒ 5 ¼ oz (150 g) 70% cocoa Guanaja chocolate from Valrhona

## Melted Chocolate Biscuit

Butter and flour a tin or an 7-inch (18-cm) square dish, 2-inch (4 to 5 cm) deep. Chop then melt the chocolate in a bain-marie*. Mix the ingredients in the order given, then add the melted chocolate. Pour into the tin. Cook at 350°F (180°C) for 25 minutes—it should look undercooked. Turn it out onto a cooling rack and remove the tin; leave to cool.

**01**

## Silky Chocolate Cream

Whip the yolks and sugar in bowl; boil the milk and cream; pour the liquid little by little on to the egg mixture while continuing to whip. Pour into a saucepan and cook as a custard to 183/185°F (84/85°C). Put the chopped chocolate into a second bowl. Pour on half of the custard, then mix. Pour on the remaining custard and mix.

**02**

Wash out the tin, butter it, and sprinkle it with sugar. Put the cooled melted chocolate biscuit in the bottom. Pour the cream over the biscuit and leave in the refrigerator for 3 hours.

## Dark Chocolate Praline

Melt the butter and cocoa paste at 110°F (45°C) in the bain-marie*. Mix the almond praline and the hazelnut paste, cocoa paste, and butter, then add the crumbled Gavottes and the cocoa nibs. Lay 5 oz (140 g) of dark chocolate praline on the cold cream. Spread, using an offset spatula, and place in the freezer.

## Chocolate Mousse

Break up the chocolate and melt it in a bain-marie*. In a second saucepan, boil the milk, then pour it on the chocolate. Mix, then add the egg yolk. Place the egg whites in a bowl and whip them energetically, while incorporating the sugar, pinch by pinch. Work the egg white, beaten to soft peaks, into the chocolate mixture. Mix gently by lifting spoonfuls from the center to the edges, while turning the bowl. Pour the mousse into the mold over the dark chocolate praline; smooth to flatten. Place in the freezer for at least 2 hours.

**05**

## Chocolate Sauce

Break the chocolate into pieces; put it in a large saucepan with the water, sugar, and cream. Bring to a boil over low heat; leave to boil over low heat, while turning with a spatula until the sauce coats the spatula and is perfectly smooth. Set aside 3 ½ oz (100 g) for the icing; keep the remainder to accompany the cake.

**06**

*To be glossy and crunchy, the chocolate must undergo a special treatment, due to the physical properties of the cocoa butter it contains. Its greatest enemy is water, which thickens it and causes irreparable damage.*

## Chocolate Icing

Grate the chocolate. Boil the cream in a saucepan, take it off the heat, and add the chocolate while stirring slowly with a spatula. Leave the mixture to cool to under 140°F (60°C) before mixing in first the butter then the chocolate sauce, stirring as little as possible. The icing must be used warm, at 95/100°F (35/40°C). Using a ladle, pour it on to the cake and spread it with a long, supple spatula. If it cools too quickly, reheat it slightly, without working it, in a warm bain-marie*.

07

## Thin Sheet of Crispy Chocolate

Chop the chocolate and melt it in the bain-marie*, over a low heat. Take it off the heat and leave to cool. In the bain-marie* reheat it very lightly while mixing (at about 87°F/31°C). On a sheet of plastic, spread a thin layer of chocolate. Just before the chocolate sets, cut a thin layer of chocolate 7 by 7 inches (18 by 18 cm). Place another sheet of plastic and a book on top to keep the chocolate from distorting. Place in the refrigerator for 45 minutes. Peel off the plastic and lay the chocolate on the cake.

08

*Keep refrigerated until ready to serve.*
*Decorate the cake with some edible gold leaves.*

# PLAISIRS, SUCRÉS

The essence of this milk chocolate, praline, and Piedmont hazelnut cake is the contrast between the milk chocolate and the varied crispy, crunchy, smooth, and melting textures—and the complex sensations they give.

# RECEIPE

MAKES 30 CAKES - Preparation time: 90 minutes - Cooking time: 60 minutes

DRINK PAIRING:
*Regular water, Corsican Muscat, a Marsala-type Italian wine such as Morce di Luce.*

**ROASTED, CRUSHED HAZELNUTS**

- ❏ 3 ½ oz (100 g) whole, raw Piedmont hazelnuts

**DACQUOISE HAZELNUT BISCUIT**

- ❏ 7 ½ oz (210 g) ground Piedmont hazelnuts
- ❏ 8 oz (230 g) confectioners sugar

- ❏ 8 egg whites (8 oz/230 g)
- ❏ 2 ½ oz (75 g) superfine sugar

**HAZELNUT PRALINE**

- ❏ 1 oz (30 g) unsalted butter
- ❏ 2 ½ oz (75 g) Jivara Valrhona cooking chocolate* (40% cocoa)
- ❏ 5 ¼ oz (150 g) hazelnut praline 60/40 (Valrhona)
- ❏ 5 ¼ oz (150 g) pure hazelnut paste (hazelnut purée)

- ❏ 5 ¼ oz (150 g) crumbled Gavottes Crispy Lace Crepes

**FINE MILK CHOCOLATE LEAVES**

- ❏ 5 ½ oz (160 g) Jivara Valrhona chocolate (40% cocoa)

**MILK CHOCOLATE GANACHE***

- ❏ 8 ¾ oz (250 g) Jivara Valrhona chocolate (40% cocoa)

- ❏ scant 1 cup (230 ml) heavy cream

**CHANTILLY MILK CHOCOLATE (TO BE MADE 12 HOURS IN ADVANCE)**

- ❏ 7 ½ oz (210 g) Jivara Valrhona chocolate (40% cocoa)
- ❏ 1 ¼ cups (300 ml) heavy cream

36

**Roasted, Crushed Hazelnuts.** On a baking sheet covered with parchment paper, spread the hazelnuts out in a single layer and roast them at 320°F (160°C) for 20 minutes. Using a sieve, remove the skins, then crush the nuts. **Dacquoise Hazelnut Biscuit.** On a dish, roast the ground hazelnuts at 300°F (150°C) for 10 minutes. Sift* the confectioners sugar and ground hazelnuts together. Beat the egg whites to stiff peaks while adding the sugar in three parts. Fold in the sifted mixture, using a spatula.

**01**

Place a frame measuring 14-by-11 inches (37 by 28 cm) and ⅓-inch (3 or 4 cm) deep on a baking sheet covered with a sheet of parchment paper or a Silpat mat. Weigh out 1 lb 8 oz (700 g) of dacquoise hazelnut biscuit and spread it evenly inside the frame using an offset spatula, then sprinkle evenly with crushed hazelnuts. Bake in a convection oven at 340°F (170°C) for approximately 30 minutes, leaving the door ajar to keep the dacquoise from rising and falling, from the concentration of steam in the oven. Once cooked, it remains both firm and soft. Leave to cool.

**02**

## Hazelnut Praline

Melt the butter and the cooking chocolate* separately at 105/110°F (40/45°C) in the bain-marie*. In the bowl of a mixer fitted with the blade, mix the hazelnut praline, the hazelnut paste, the cooking chocolate, and the butter. Add the crumbled gavottes.

03

Weigh out 1 lb 3 oz (550 g) of hazelnut praline, lay it on the dacquoise hazelnut biscuit in the frame, and flatten using an angled spatula. Store in the refrigerator.

Remove the frame from the dacquoise hazelnut biscuit and hazelnut praline and cut into rectangles measuring 4-by-1 inch (10 by 2.5 cm). Store in the freezer.

04

05

**Fine Milk Chocolate Leaves.** On a 8-by-12 inch (20 by 30 cm) sheet of plastic, spread the softened milk chocolate. As soon as the chocolate sets, mark it into 4-by-1 inch (10 by 2.5 cm) rectangles. Lay a leaf of plastic and a weight over it before placing in the refrigerator to set.

**Milk Chocolate Ganache.** Chop the chocolate. Boil the cream and pour it on to the chocolate; mix. Pour into a dish and let set at room temperature.

**06**

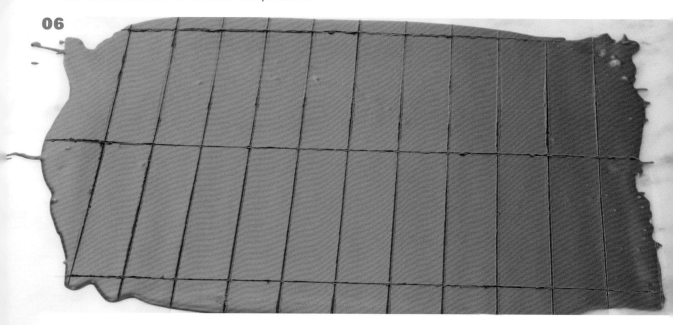

Place the rectangles of fine milk chocolate leaves (shiny side down) on a baking sheet covered with a sheet of parchment paper. Using a pastry bag fitted with a railroad nozzle and filled with milk chocolate ganache, cover the rectangles from end to end, lengthwise. Place a second rectangle on top, and repeat the procedure. Do not put a chocolate rectangle on the second layer of ganache. Store in the freezer.

**07**

*Keep refrigerated until eaten. It is very important to sample this cake cold!*

## Chantilly Milk Chocolate

Chop the chocolate. Boil the cream and pour it onto the chocolate. Mix. Pour into a dish and leave in the refrigerator for approximately 12 hours.

In a bowl, whip the mixture. Fill a plastic pastry bag fitted with a stainless steel No. 12 nozzle with chantilly milk chocolate. Pipe* two thin lines of Chantilly on a rectangle of dacquoise hazelnut biscuit and hazelnut praline, and lay a milk chocolate and ganache rectangle on top.

Pipe two thick lines of chantilly milk chocolate, side by side. Finish by placing a rectangle of milk chocolate (shiny side up) on top.

## 09

*These cakes will keep in the refrigerator for 24 hours.*

# TARTE FINE CHLOÉ

This tart is composed of cornmeal shortcrust pastry, pieces of raspberry, and shavings of Manjari 64% cocoa chocolate ganache for its bitter taste, then covered with a thin sheet of dark chocolate with fleur de sel.

# RECEIPE

SERVES 8 - Preparation time: 60 minutes - Cooking time: 60 minutes

## SHORTCRUST PASTRY MADE WITH CORNMEAL

- ❐ 5 ¼ oz (150 g) unsalted butter
- ❐ 1 oz (30 g) ground almonds
- ❐ 3 ¼ oz (90 g) confectioners sugar
- ❐ pinch (½ g) vanilla powder
- ❐ 1 whole egg (2 oz/60 g)
- ❐ pinch (½ g) Guerande fleur de sel
- ❐ 8 oz (225 g) sifted flour*
- ❐ 1 ½ oz (45 g) cornmeal

## CHLOÉ'S CHOCOLATE GANACHE

- ❐ 1 ¼ oz (35 g) unsalted butter
- ❐ 5 ¼ oz (150 g) Manjari Valrhona 64% cooking chocolate*
- ❐ 5 oz (140 g) raspberry purée

## DARK CHOCOLATE LEAVES AND TRIANGLES (MAKE 24 HOURS BEFOREHAND)

- ❐ 8 ¾ oz (250 g) Jivara Valrhona dark chocolate (64% cocoa)

## DRIED RASPBERRIES

- ❐ 5 ¼ oz (150 g) fresh raspberries

44

## Shortcrust Pastry Made with Cornmeal

In the bowl of a mixer fitted with the blade, knead the butter and add the ingredients in the order given. Mix as little as possible. Wrap in plastic and store in the refrigerator for 30 minutes. Roll out the pastry and prick it. Butter a baking ring 8-inch (21-cm) in diameter and 1-inch (2-cm) high, and cut a disk of pastry in that size. Place it on a baking sheet covered with parchment paper and leave in the refrigerator for an hour. Bake in a convection oven at 340°F (170°C) for approximately 15 minutes.

**01**

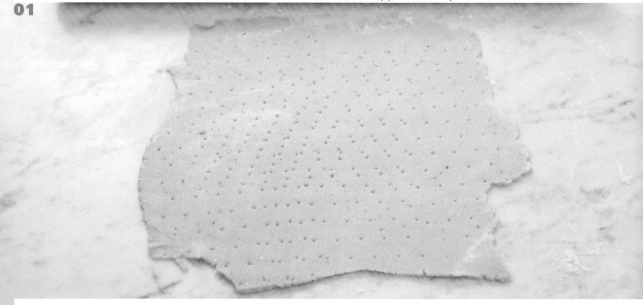

## Chloé's Chocolate Ganache

Keep the butter at room temperature. Melt the cooking chocolate* in the microwave or in a bain-marie*. Heat the raspberry purée, pour a third of it over the cooking chocolate, and mix, starting from the center and then widening the movement, little by little, toward the outside. Repeat the procedure twice with the remainder of the purée and then stir in the butter at 100°F (40°C). Emulsify* the ganache using a hand blender and use immediately.

**02**

**Leaves and Triangles of Dark Chocolate**
Melt the chocolate, temper* it on marble, and pour it on to a sheet of "guitar" paper*.

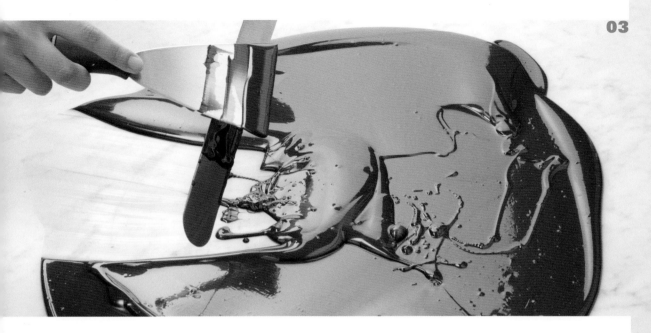

Spread the chocolate out using an angled spatula, lay a second sheet of "guitar" paper* on top, and finish spreading it, using a rolling pin.

Let the chocolate crystallize* slightly. Then, using a knife, draw on it a circle 8-inch (21-cm) in diameter and cut it into eight. Place a sheet of parchment paper and a weight on it to keep the chocolate from deforming. Let it cool for 24 hours in the refrigerator.

**Dried Raspberries**

Preheat the convection oven to 195°F (90°C). Spread the raspberries on a baking sheet covered with parchment paper. Bake and allow to dry for about an hour and a half.

**05**

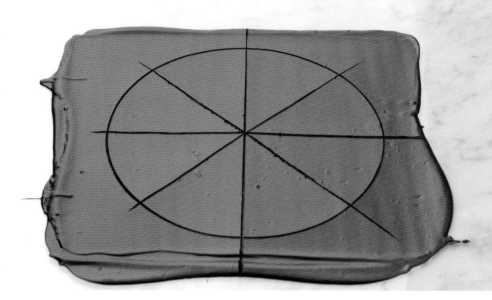

Using a rolling pin, lightly crush the dried raspberries. Lay the circle on a baking sheet covered with a sheet of parchment paper. Place the cooked cornmeal pastry ring in it, and sprinkle with dried raspberries. Pour 10 ½ oz (300 g) of Chloé's chocolate ganache on top, and leave it to set in the refrigerator for 2 hours. Decorate each part of the tart with a triangle of dark chocolate.

**06**

*Serve at the room temperature.*

Using a hot knife, mark out eight triangles.

## 07

Decorate each part of the tart with a triangle of dark chocolate.

*The tart will keep for 2 days in the refrigerator.*

# TARTE INFINIMENT VANILLE

This tart is made up of a shortcrust pastry base topped with white chocolate and vanilla ganache and vanilla mascarpone cream. Pierre Hermé has chosen to unite vanilla pods from different origins: from Tahiti for their intense background note, from Mexico for a floral note, and from Madagascar for a woody note. This association allows him to create a vanilla *maison*, to express his own interpretation of vanilla.

# RECEIPE

**SERVES 6 TO 8 - Preparation time: 120 minutes - Cooking time: 90 minutes**

DRINK PAIRING:
*Vanilla tea, Jardin de Pierre tea, Sencha green tea.*

## SHORTCRUST PASTRY

- ❐ 2 ½ oz (75 g) unsalted butter
- ❐ ½ oz (15 g) ground almonds
- ❐ 1 ¾ oz (50 g) confectioners sugar
- ❐ pinch (½ g) vanilla powder
- ❐ ½ egg (1 oz/30 g)
- ❐ A pinch Guerande fleur de sel
- ❐ 4 ½ oz (125 g) flour

## SPOON BISCUIT

- ❐ 1 oz (25 g) flour
- ❐ 1 oz (25 g) potato starch
- ❐ 2 eggs separated (3½ oz/100g)
- ❐ 1 ½ oz (45 g) superfine sugar
- ❐ 2 egg yolks (1 ½ oz/45 g)

## VANILLA CUSTARD

- ❐ Sheets of Gold Quality gelatine leaves (200 Blooms)
- ❐ 1 Madagascar vanilla pod, split and scraped
- ❐ 1 cup (250 ml) heavy cream
- ❐ 2 egg yolks (50 g/1 ¾ oz)
- ❐ 2 oz (65 g) superfine sugar

## VANILLA-FLAVORED MARSCAPONE CREAM

- ❐ 5 ¼ oz (150 g) mascarpone cheese
- ❐ (8 oz) vanilla custard

## VANILLA GANACHE

- ❐ 4 ½ oz (125 g) white chocolate

- ❐ 1½ Madagascar vanilla pod, split and scraped
- ❐ scant ½ cup (115 ml) heavy cream
- ❐ few drops (2 g) natural vanilla extract, without alcohol
- ❐ pinch (½ g) vanilla powder

## VANILLA ICING

- ❐ 1 ¾ oz (50 g) white chocolate
- ❐ 1 tablespoon (15 g) superfine sugar
- ❐ A pinch pectin* NH for jam
- ❐ 2 tablespoons (30 ml) heavy cream
- ❐ 2 tablespoons (30 ml) mineral water
- ❐ ¼ Madagascar vanilla pod, split and scraped

- ❐ A large pinch powdered titanium oxide* (from drugstore)

## VANILLA SYRUP

- ❐ 1½ Madagascar vanilla pods, split and scraped
- ❐ 1 ¾ oz (50 g) superfine sugar
- ❐ 6 ½ tablespoons (100 ml) mineral water
- ❐ few drops (2 g) natural vanilla extract, without alcohol
- ❐ 1 teaspoon (5 g) Old Brown "Agricultural" rum

## FINISH

- ❐ Vanilla powder

52

## Shortcrust Pastry

Knead the butter and in then stir the ingredients one by one. Keep in the refrigerator under plastic. On a floure[d] work surface, roll out the dough to a thickness of about $^1/_{10}$-inch (2 mm). Cut out a disk 9-inch (23-cm) in diamete[r] Put it in the refrigerator for 30 minutes. Butter a pastry ring 7-inch (17-cm) in diameter and 1-inch (2-cm) high, line [it] with pastry* and cut off any excess. Lay the ring on a baking sheet covered with parchment paper and line* it wit[h] aluminum foil. Fill with dried beans and bake in a convection oven at 340°F (170°C) for approximately 25 minute[s]

**01**

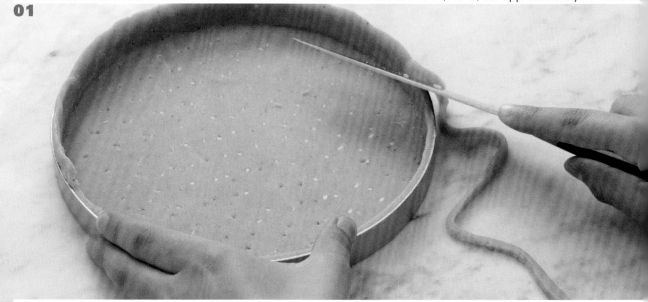

## Spoon Biscuit

Sift* the flour and potato starch. Beat the egg whites with the sugar, to create stiff peaks. Pour the yolks into the whites, stir gently for a few seconds, and then stop. Stir the flour and potato starch by lifting the preparation gently, using a spatula. Using a pastry bag fitted with a No. 7 nozzle, on parchment paper, draw a disk 5-inch (13-cm) in diameter. Bake in a convection oven at 450°F (230°C) for approximately 6 minutes. Remove from the oven and leave to cool.

**02**

## Vanilla Custard

Soak the gelatine in cold water for 20 minutes and infuse the vanilla pods in the boiled cream for 30 minutes. Pass this infusion through a chinois*. Mix the yolks with the sugar, bring the vanilla cream to a boil, and pour it over the yolks and sugar. Whip and return to the pan before bringing to 180°F (85°C). Run a finger along the back of a spatula coated with cream; it's ready if the track remains visible. Add the drained gelatine, blend, allow to cool, and store in the refrigerator.

**03**

## Vanilla-flavored Marscapone Cream

In the bowl of a mixer fitted with the whisk, whip the marscapone lightly until fluffy*, then dilute it progressively with part of the vanilla custard, then the remainder, and let it rise. Use immediately.

Use a pastry bag to fill an 8-inch (20-cm) diameter ring, ¾-inch (1.5-cm) high, after you have dipped it in hot water and drained it. Smooth with a spatula. Turn out at once and place in the freezer. Once completely frozen, you can use it.

**04**                                                                                         **05**

*The ring should be neither too hot nor too cold. If the circle is too hot, your cream will become liquid, if it is too cold, it will not turn out neatly.*

55

## Vanilla Ganache.

Melt the chocolate in a bain-marie*. Heat the vanilla with the cream to approximately 120°F (50°C); let it infuse for 30 minutes. Boil the cream with the vanilla extract and powder. Pour the cream over the cooking chocolate*, while mixing. Blend and use immediately.

## Vanilla Icing.

Melt the chocolate in a bain-marie*. Mix the sugar with the pectin*. Boil the cream, water, and vanilla. Remove the vanilla and add the sugar/pectin mixture*. Boil, pour it over the chocolate, and stir. Add the titanium oxide* powder. Blend and use immediately.

**06**  **07**

## Vanilla Syrup

Split and scrape the vanilla pods, put them in the sugar and water, bring to a boil, and let it infuse for at least 30 minutes. Add the liquid vanilla extract and rum. Store in an airtight container in the refrigerator. The vanilla pods can remain in the syrup.

In the shortcrust pastry base, pour the vanilla ganache to reach three fifths of its depth. Using a brush, dampen the spoon biscuit with the vanilla syrup, lay it on top, and press gently.

**08**

*The tart will keep in the refrigerator for 2 days.*

Decorate with vanilla ganache and place in the refrigerator. Once the ganache is set, place the tart on a baking sheet of the correct size.

## 09

Heat the vanilla icing to 95°F (35°C). Take the mascarpone cream disk from the freezer, place it on a rack, then, using a ladle, pour the vanilla icing over it and smooth it with an offset spatula so as to obtain a thin, even layer.

Scrape the underside with an offset spatula and place it on the frozen ganache, taking care to center it. Using a tea strainer, sprinkle approximately ¾-inch (2-cm) of the left side with vanilla powder.

## 10

*Keep refrigerated until eaten.*

# ÉMOTION
# ENVIE

Emotion: Envy is a light and fruity creation composed of black currant compote, crème brûlée, and violet mascarpone cream, decorated with a macaron. The sweetness of the violet just emphasizes the strength of the black currants.

# RECIPE

**MAKES 10 GLASSES · Preparation time: 90 minutes · Cooking time: 180 minutes**

DRINK PAIRING:
*Mineral water, black Ceylon tea, Corsican Muscat.*

## POACHED BLACK CURRANTS

- ⅔ cup (150 ml) mineral water
- 3 oz (80 g) superfine sugar
- 5 ¼ oz (150 g) black currants (fresh or frozen)

## BLACK CURRANT AND CASSIS COMPOTE (MAKE 12 HOURS IN ADVANCE)

- ½ oz (11 g) Gold Quality gelatine leaves (200 Blooms)
- 1 lb 1 oz (500 g) black currant purée
- 3 ¼ oz (90 g) red currant purée
- 4 oz (115 g) superfine sugar

- 1 ¾ oz (150 g) poached black currants

## JOCONDE BISCUIT

- 1 oz (30 g) unsalted butter
- 6 oz (150 g) ground almonds
- 4 ¼ oz (120 g) confectioners sugar
- 4 whole eggs (7 oz/200 g)
- 4 egg whites (4 ¾ oz/130 g)
- ½ oz (20 g) superfine sugar
- 1 ¼ oz (40 g) T55 flour

## VIOLET VANILLA CRÈME BRÛLÉE

- 1 oz (24 g) Gold Quality gelatine leaves (200 Blooms)
- 1 quart (1 L) fresh whole milk

- 9 ¾ oz (280 g) superfine sugar
- 1 small (4 g) Madagascar vanilla pod
- 1 quart (1 L) heavy cream
- few drops (2 g) violet flavoring
- 24 egg yolks (17 oz/480 g)

## VIOLET VANILLA CUSTARD

- ¼ oz (3 g) Gold Quality gelatine leaves (200 Blooms)
- 1 small (3 g) Madagascar vanilla pod
- 1 cup (250 ml) heavy cream
- 2 egg yolks (50 g/1 ¾ oz)
- 2 oz (60 g) superfine sugar
- few drops (2 g) violet flavoring

## VIOLET VANILLA MARSCAPONE CREAM

- 7 oz (200 g) mascarpone

## JASMINE AND CORNFLOWER MACARON

- 10 ½ oz (300 g) confectioners sugar
- 10 ½ oz (300 g) ground almonds
- 7 egg whites (7 ½ oz/220 g)
- 75 ml (⅓ cup) mineral water
- 10 ½ oz (300 g) superfine sugar
- Dried cornflower petals

## FINISH

- Fresh blueberries

### Poached Black Currants

Boil the water with the sugar and pour it over the black currants. Pour into an airtight container and leave to macerate in the refrigerator overnight. The day before using, drain the fruit and store in the refrigerator.

### Black Currant and Cassis Compote

Soak the gelatine in cold water for 20 minutes. Mix the fruit purées and the sugar. Drain the gelatine and soften it in the microwave; stir in the purée, whisking. Add the poached black currants and set aside.

**01**
**02**

### Joconde Biscuit

Melt the butter. Put the ground almonds and confectioners sugar into the bowl of a mixer fitted with the whisk, pour in half of the eggs, and beat for 8 minutes. Add the remaining eggs in two batches and beat for 10 to 12 minutes. Pour a little of this mixture into the melted butter and whisk. Beat the egg whites with the superfine sugar to form stiff peaks, and pour it on the first preparation. Add the flour in a steady stream and stir gently before incorporating the butter into the mixture.

**03**

*To soften the gelatine, put a bowl of water in the refrigerator.*
*Separate the leaves one by one and let them soak for 20 minutes.*

On a Silpat mat* 12-by-16 inches (30 by 40 cm), using an angled offset spatula, spread 1 lb 2 oz (530 g) of joconde biscuit. Bake in a convection oven at 450°F (230 °C) for 5 minutes. Turn over and peel off the mat. Leave to cool. Be careful not to brown the biscuit too much during cooking.

Using a cutter, cut out disks measuring 2-inch (4.5-cm) in diameter. Store them in an airtight container in the refrigerator.

**04**

**05**

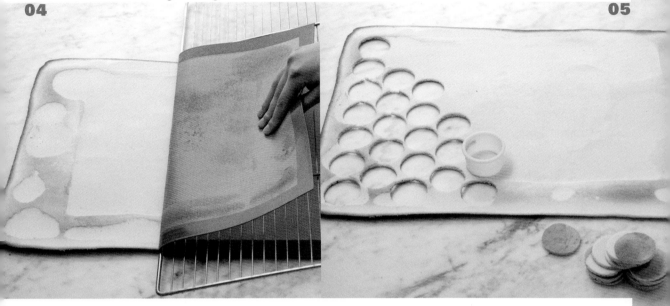

**Violet Vanilla Crème Brulée.** Preheat the oven to 200°F (90°C). Soak the gelatine in cold water for 20 minutes. Boil the milk, the sugar, and the split and scraped vanilla pod, and let the mixture infuse for 20 minutes. Strain through a chinois* and add the drained gelatine. Mix the cream, the violet flavoring, and the egg yolks with the flavored milk. Pour 1½ oz (40 g) of vanilla violet Crème Brûlée into each glass. Bake for approximately 30 minutes. Shake the glasses lightly: the center should be set. If they are not, continue cooking for 5 minutes. Remove the glasses from the oven, allow to cool and then store them in the fridge.

**06**

### Violet Vanilla Custard

Soak the gelatine in cold water for 20 minutes. Infuse the split and scraped vanilla pod in the cream for 30 minutes. Pass this infusion through a chinois*. Mix the yolks with the sugar, bring the cream to a boil, and pour it over the yolks. Whip and return to the saucepan to cook as a custard to 180°F (85°C). Add the drained gelatine and the violet flavoring, then blend and store to cool in a container in the refrigerator.

**07**

### Violet Vanilla Marscapone Cream

In the bowl of a mixer fitted with the whisk, beat the mascarpone to make it homogenous. Add the violet vanilla custard in three batches and beat well. Use immediately.

**08**

**Jasmine and Cornflower Macaron**

Prepare a macaron (see Macaron Mogador, p. 97). On a baking tray covered with a Silpat mat*, using a 2-inch (5.5-cm) diameter stencil, form the macaron disks and scrape them using an angled offset spatula. Immediately sprinkle with dried cornflower petals and leave for 4 hours to form a crust. Bake in a convection oven at 175°F (80°C) for 2 hours, leaving the oven door ajar.

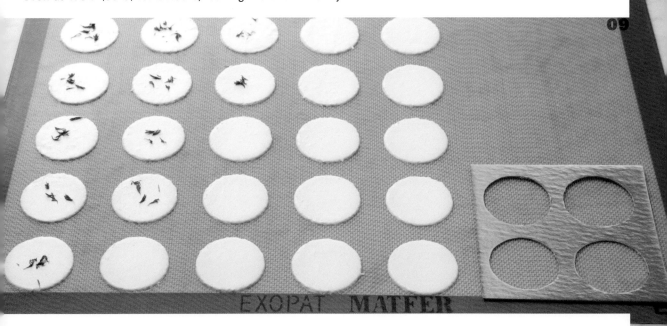

In a tall glass of violet vanilla crème brûlée, pour in 1 ¾ oz (50 g) of black currant and cassis compote, and add a disk of Joconde biscuit. Allow to set for 2 hours in the refrigerator. Using a disposable pastry bag, garnish with 25 g (1 oz) of violet vanilla marscapone cream. On top of the violet vanilla marscapone cream, arrange 3 fresh blueberries. Place a disk of jasmine and cornflower macaron on the glass.

*Keep refrigerated until ready to serve.*
*These glasses will keep in the refrigerator for 24 hours.*

# SURPRISE CÉLESTE

This sweet and crispy meringue conceals a tart, melting heart. It's the pleasure of a new taste, a mixture of strawberry and rhubarb, well known to lovers of German pastries and associated with passion fruit. Brought together, they form a sort of north/south alliance, both smooth and sharp at the same time.

# RECICE

DRINK PAIRING:

*Gewurztraminer Vendanges Tardives, Champagne Duval-Leroy Rosé de Saignée, Vouvray Demi-sec.*

## FRENCH MERINGUE

- ❏ 3 egg whites (4 oz/100 g)
- ❏ 7 ½ oz (200 g) superfine sugar

## ALMOND BISCUITS WITH SLIVERED ALMONDS

- ❏ 3 oz (75 g) ground white almonds
- ❏ 9 ½ oz (275 g) superfine sugar
- ❏ 1 oz (20 g) T55 flour
- ❏ 4 egg whites (4 ½ oz/125 g)

- ❏ 1 ¾ oz (50 g) flaked almonds

## PURÉE OF RHUBARB CONFIT (PREPARE 12 HOURS IN ADVANCE)

- ❏ 8 ¾ oz (250 g) rhubarb, frozen or chilled, in pieces
- ❏ 1½ oz (40 g) superfine sugar
- ❏ 1 oz (25 g) lemon juice
- ❏ A pinch powdered cloves

## RHUBARB CONFIT WITH STRAWBERRIES

- ❏ ¼ oz (9 g) Gold Quality gelatine leaves (200 Blooms)
- ❏ 3 ½ oz (100 g) rhubarb confit
- ❏ 10 ½ oz (300 g) of fresh strawberry purée
- ❏ 1 oz (30 g) superfine sugar

## PASSION FRUIT CREAM (PREPARE 24 HOURS IN ADVANCE)

- ❏ 3 whole eggs (5 ¼ oz/150 g)

- ❏ 5 oz (140 g) superfine sugar
- ❏ 3 ½ oz (105 g) passion fruit juice (approximately 5 fruits)
- ❏ ½ oz (15 g) lemon juice
- ❏ 5 ¼ oz (150 g) unsalted butter

## PASSION FRUIT CHIFFON CREAM

- ❏ 5 ¼ oz (150 g) unsalted butter
- ❏ 1 lb 1 oz (500 g) passion fruit cream

**68**

## French Meringue

Pour the egg whites into the bowl of a mixer fitted with the whisk; whip at medium speed, until they double in volume, incorporating 1½ oz (35 g) of sugar, and continue to whisk until they become very firm, very smooth, and very glossy, while adding 2½ oz (65 g) of sugar. Detach the mixer bowl and fold in 3½ oz (100 g) of sugar in a steady stream, lifting the meringue with a spatula, and working it as little as possible. Use immediately.

**01**

## Meringue Shells

Fill a plastic pastry bag with the meringue and pipe it one-third of way up the cups of the dome-shaped 2½-inch (7-cm) Flexipan molds then, using a spoon, cover the domes. Scrape off any excess meringue, with a spoon. Ideally, dry the meringue shells in the oven at 140°F (60°C) for several hours. When they are completely dried, turn them out on to a baking sheet covered with a sheet of parchment paper and return to the oven at 230°F (110°C) for 20 minutes.

**02**

*Ideally use old\* egg whites that have been kept at room temperature: They are more liquid, they beat better, and they do not fall so easily.*

## Almond Biscuits with Slivered Almonds

Mix and sift* the ground almonds with 7 oz (200 g) superfine sugar and the flour. In the bowl of a mixer fitted with the whisk, beat the egg whites to stiff peaks, adding the rest of the superfine sugar little by little. Remove the bowl from the mixer and fold in the first mixture by hand, lifting it gently. Using a pastry bag fitted with a No. 8 nozzle, form disks 2 ¼-inch (6-cm) in diameter, and sprinkle with flaked almonds. Cook at 340°F (170°C) for 20 minutes. Leave to cool.

03

E 06

## Purée of Rhubarb Confit

The day before, cut the fresh rhubarb into ½-inch (1.5-cm) sections and leave them to macerate in the sugar.

04

Drain the rhubarb and cook it to a purée with the lemon juice and powdered cloves. Leave to cool, then blend. Use immediately or store in an airtight container in the refrigerator or freezer.

**05**

**Rhubarb Confit with Strawberries**
Soak the gelatine in cold water for at least 20 minutes. Drain it and dissolve it in a little rhubarb confit. Add the strawberry purée and the sugar, then stir. Pour into a rectangular dish and leave in the freezer for an hour.
Using a cutter, cut out disks measuring 2-inch (4-cm) in diameter.

**06**

**Passion Fruit Cream**

Mix the eggs, the superfine sugar, the passion fruit juice, and the lemon juice.
Cook in a bain-marie*, stirring occasionally. Bring this mixture to 178/180°F (83/84°C).

07

Pass it through a chinois*, cool to 140°F (60°C) in the bain-marie* and add the butter, using a whisk. Mix it all with a hand blender for 10 minutes, so as to burst the fat molecules and obtain the desired creamy result. Leave to cool for 24 hours before use.

08

**Passion Fruit Chiffon Cream**

In the bowl of a mixer fitted first with the blade, then the whisk, whip the butter to make it as fluffy* as possible. Now work in the passion fruit cream. This preparation must be made and used immediately.

**09**

**Assembly**

Put the meringue shells back into the Flexipans and half-fill with the passion fruit chiffon cream. Arrange the disk of rhubarb and strawberry confit on top, pressing lightly, and garnish to the top with passion fruit chiffon cream, so as to fill the meringue shell.

**10**

Arrange the almond biscuit with slivered almonds on it. Keep in the refrigerator to make turning out and wrapping easier.

**11**

Lay a sheet of red cellophane (9-by-10 inches/23 by 25 cm) on the work surface, then place a Surprise in the center, upside down (curved side down), fold back the two longer opposite sides of the cellophane so that they come together under the Surprise, and turn in the ends, in the opposite direction. Repeat with the remaining surprises.

**12**

*You should wrap the cake when it is very cold, almost frozen.*

*Keep refrigerated until ready to serve.*

# MISS GLA'GLA MONTEBELLO

Individual ice-cream confections in an elongated rectangular shape: the fruity taste shines. This composition plays on the association between strawberry sorbet and pistachio ice, with notes of roasted pistachios.

# RECEIPE

**PISTACHIO MACARONS**

- ❑ 10 ½ oz (300 g) confectioners sugar
- ❑ 10 ½ oz (300 g) ground almonds
- ❑ 1 drop pistachio-green dye
- ❑ 1 drop of lemon-yellow dye
- ❑ 7 egg whites (200 g/ 7 oz)
- ❑ ⅓ cup (75 ml) mineral water

- ❑ 10 ½ oz (300 g) superfine sugar

**STRAWBERRY SORBET (PREPARE 24 HOURS IN ADVANCE)**

- ❑ whipping cream
- ❑ 6 ¾ oz (190 g) superfine sugar
- ❑ 6 tablespoons (90 ml) mineral water

- ❑ 1 lb 6 oz (650 g) strawberries
- ❑ 1 tablespoon (15 ml) lemon juice

**PISTACHIO ICE CREAM (PREPARE 24 HOURS IN ADVANCE)**

- ❑ 1 ½ cups (350 ml) whole milk
- ❑ 1 oz (30 g) milk powder

- ❑ 2 oz (55 g) pistachio paste*
- ❑ 6 ½ tablespoons (100 ml) whipping cream
- ❑ 3 ½ oz (100 g) superfine sugar
- ❑ 2 egg yolks (1 ¾ oz/50 g)
- ❑ 1 ¼ oz (35 g) pistachio nuts, blanched and toasted

78

## Pistachio Macarons

Sift* the confectioners sugar and the ground almonds together. Mix the colorings into half of the egg whites. Stir in the sifted preparation. Boil the water and sugar to 245°F (118°C). Start to beat the second half of the egg whites to form stiff peaks. Pour the sugar solution on to the beaten egg whites. Whisk and let cool to 120°F (50°C) before incorporating the first preparation. Beat, while allowing the mixture to fall back. Using a stencil, arrange macaron rectangles on a tray covered with a Silpat mat*.

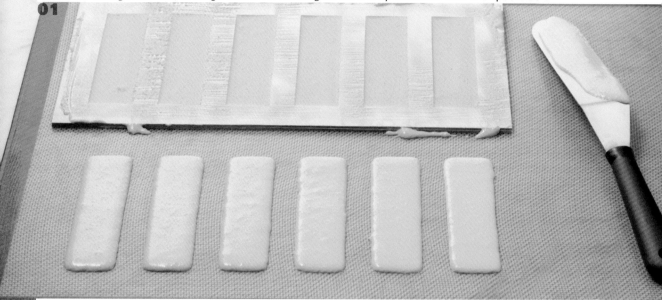

Remove the stencil. Leave the rectangles to form a crust, for about an hour at room temperature. Bake in a convection oven at 325°F (160°C) for 8 minutes, quickly opening and closing the oven door. Leave to cool.

*To make the stencil for the macarons, cut 6 cardboard rectangles 1½ by 5 inches (3.5 by 12 cm).*

## Strawberry Sorbet

Boil the cream and pour it on to the superfine sugar. Blend first while it is hot, then store in the refrigerator. Blend the strawberries to obtain a puree and pass it through a chinois*. After allowing it to mature for approximately 24 hours, add the strawberry pulp and the lemon juice to the syrup. Blend a second time before churning.

03

## Pistachio Ice Cream

Heat the milk, the milk powder, the pistachio paste*, the cream, and the sugar to 95°F (35°C), then add the egg yolk, and bring to 100°F (40°C). Cook at 180°F (85°C), as a custard. Let the mixture rest for 24 hours in the refrigerator, pass it through the chinois*, blend, and churn. Stir in the blanched, toasted pistachios at the end of churning.

04

## Montebello Mixture

Place the pistachio ice cream on the strawberry sorbet in a chilled stainless steel tray.

Gently mix the two together using an ice-cream scoop in order to obtain a marbled effect.

**05**

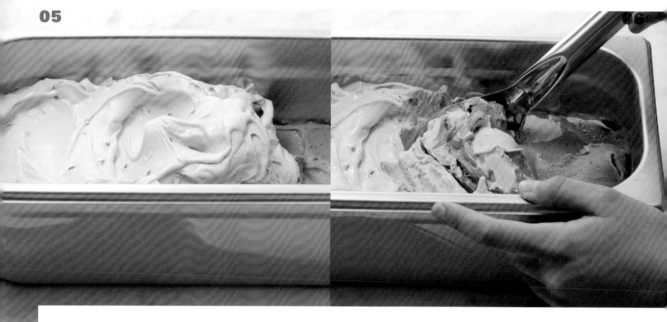

In a stainless steel frame (22 ½ by 4 ½ inches/57 by 11 cm) and 1-inch (2.5-cm) deep, placed on a baking sheet covered with a sheet of parchment paper, arrange the mixture. Leave in the freezer for at least 45 minutes.

**07**

Cut the ice cream into rectangles measuring 1 ¼ by 4 ½ inches (3 by 11.5 cm). Store in the freezer.

Place a rectangle of the ice cream between two rectangles of pistachio macaron.
Store in the freezer.

## 09

*Remove from the freezer 30 minutes before serving.*
*The preparations will keep for 8 weeks in the freezer.*

This is a composition in which the creaminess of mascarpone and olive oil, punctuated with pieces of dried black olives, reaches a sort of climax that's difficult to describe... but that we want to share! The puff pastry is rendered crisp by very fast baking, while the taste of tomato gives the dish a surprising and original touch.

# RÉVÉLATIONS
## (TOMATO/STRAWBERRY/OLIVE OIL)

# RECURE

DRINK PAIRING:
*Sauternes, Sainte-Croix-du-Mont, Vouvray Moelleux.*

**PUFF PASTRY
WITH TOMATO**

- ❒ 17 ½ oz (490 g) butter
- ❒ 15 oz (425 g) T55 flour
- ❒ 2 oz (60 g) tomato powder
  (Oliviers & Co.)
- ❒ 1 oz (18 g) fleur de sel
- ❒ ⅔ cup (150 ml) mineral
  water
- ❒ A few drops white vinegar
- ❒ superfine sugar

**JOCONDE BISCUIT**

- ❒ 1 oz (30 g) unsalted butter
- ❒ 12 oz (150 g) ground
  almonds
- ❒ 12 oz (120 g) confectioners
  sugar
- ❒ 3 whole eggs (8 oz/200 g)
- ❒ 4 egg whites (4 ¾ oz/130 g)
- ❒ 1 oz (20 g) superfine sugar
- ❒ 1½ oz (40 g) T55 flour

**TOMATO AND
STRAWBERRY COMPOTE**

- ❒ 1 oz (25 g) Gold Quality
  gelatine leaves
  (200 Blooms)
- ❒ 1 lb 14 oz (850 g) tomatoes

- ❒ 5 ¼ oz (150 g) fresh
  strawberry puree
- ❒ 5 ¼ oz (150 g) superfine
  sugar
- ❒ 100 ml (6 ½ tablespoons)
  lemon juice

**DRIED BLACK OLIVES
(PREPARE 12 HOURS
IN ADVANCE)**

- ❒ 1½ oz (40 g) pitted black
  Greek olives, without
  spices

**MASCARPONE CREAM
WITH OLIVE OIL
AND VANILLA**

- ❒ ¼ oz (3 g) Gold Quality
  gelatine leaves
  (200 Blooms)
- ❒ ¼ cup (65 ml) heavy cream
- ❒ 2 oz (60 g) superfine sugar
- ❒ 1½ Madagascar vanilla
  pods
- ❒ 6 ¼ oz (175 g) Ravida olive
  oil (Oliviers & Co.)
- ❒ 8 ¾ oz (250 g) mascarpone

## Puff Pastry with Tomato

Work 14 oz (350 g) butter, 3 oz (75 g) flour, and the tomato powder together so that they are completely blended. Form into a flattened ball and wrap in plastic before putting in the refrigerator for an hour. Loosen it by mixing in the rest of the flour and butter, the fleur de sel, water, and vinegar. Rewrap in plastic and let it rest for an hour.

**01**

Roll out the pastry lengthwise, giving it two double turns at 2 hour intervals and leaving the pastry in the refrigerator after every turn, then give a single turn before rolling out. Roll out the pastry. Dampen it lightly on both sides and turn it over in the superfine sugar. Put it in the refrigerator. Then, using a knife, mark out strips measuring 3-by-¾ inches (8 by 2 cm). Leave to rest for 3 to 4 hours. Lay the strips on a tray covered with parchment paper. Cook at 340°F (170°C) for 12 to 15 minutes.

**02**

*You can store this puff pastry in the refrigerator for several days after having done the two double turns.*

**Joconde Biscuit**

Make a Joconde biscuit (see Emotion: Envy, p. 62).

On a Silpat mat* 12-by-16 inches (30 by 40 cm), using an angled offset spatula, spread 21 oz (530 g) of Joconde biscuit. Bake in a convection oven at 450°F (230°C) for 5 minutes. Turn out on a sheet of parchment paper and peel off the mat; leave to cool. Be careful not to let the biscuit brown too much during cooking.

**03**

**Tomato and Strawberry Compote**

Soak the gelatine in cold water for at least 20 minutes. Peel the tomatoes by plunging them into boiling water for a minute. Purée them. Warm a quarter of the tomato purée at 110°F (45°C) to dissolve the gelatine; stir in the remaining tomato purée, then the strawberry purée, the sugar, and the lemon juice, whisking energetically.

**04**

Pour 10 oz (250 g) of compote into the bottom of a 8-inch (19-cm) diameter dish.

**Dried Black Olives**

Cut the olives in half and dry them for 12 hours in an oven at 195°F (90°C). Chop them roughly and store in an airtight container.

**05**

**Mascarpone Cream with Olive Oil and Vanilla**

Soak the gelatine in cold water for 20 minutes. Boil the cream with the sugar and the split and scraped vanilla pods. Leave to infuse for 20 minutes, then remove the vanilla pods. Drain the gelatine, add it to the warm cream, and mix. Pour the mixture into a food processor and trickle in the olive oil slowly, to obtain a conistency similar to mayonnaise. Mix in the mascarpone, then the chopped olives, and mix gently with a spatula.

**06**

## Assembly

Lay the disk of Joconde biscuit on top of the tomato and strawberry compote. Leave to cool. Spread it with 8 oz (200 g) of marscapone cream with olive oil and dried black olives. Cover the surface with strips of puff pastry with tomato, and garnish again with 8 oz (200 g) of marscapone cream with olive oil and dried black olives. Place in the refrigerator for at least an hour. Decorate with halved cherry tomatoes and halved strawberries. Finish off with 6 strips of puff pastry with tomato.

*Keep refrigerated until ready to serve.*

# MACARON
# MOGADOR

This macaron is crisp on the outside, creamy and fluffy on the inside. In the ganache, the milk chocolate softens the acidity of the passion fruit, which brings out the flavors.

# RECISE

## PASSSION FRUIT AND MILK CHOCOLATE GANACHE

- ❏ 3 ½ oz (100 g) unsalted butter, at room temperature
- ❏ 1 lb 3 oz (550 g) Jivara Valrhona chocolate, or 40% cocoa milk chocolate

- ❏ 10 passion fruits (for 1 cup /250 ml juice)
- ❏ Cocoa powder

## PASSION FRUIT MACARON

- ❏ 10 ½ oz (300 g) confectioners sugar
- ❏ 10 ½ oz (300 g) ground almonds
- ❏ A few drops yellow food coloring

- ❏ 2 to 3 drops red food coloring
- ❏ 7 egg whites (7 ¾ oz/220 g)
- ❏ ⅓ cup (75 ml) mineral water
- ❏ 10 ½ oz (300 g) superfine sugar

**Passsion fruit and Milk Chocolate Ganache**
Cut the butter into pieces and chop the chocolate with a serrated knife.
Cut the passion fruits in half, empty them using a small spoon, and sieve* the flesh to obtain 1 cup (250 ml) of juice. Bring it to a boil. Melt half the chopped chocolate in a bain-marie*. Pour the hot juice onto the chocolate in three batches.

**01**

Once the temperature of the mixture reaches 140°F (60°C), incorporate the butter, little by little. Mix until the ganache is smooth. Pour into a gratin dish. Lay a sheet of plastic over it, touching the surface of the ganache. Keep it in the refrigerator until it becomes creamy.

**02**

*If the ganache separates when you pour in the passion fruit juice, this is normal. The molecules of fat in the chocolate are dividing. Simply continue to mix, as explained in the recipe, and you'll get a nice, creamy, shiny ganache.*

## Passion Fruit Macaron

Sieve* the confectioners sugar and the ground almonds. Mix the colorings into half of the egg whites. Work them into the sugar almond mixture. Boil the water and superfine sugar to 245°F (118°C). As soon as the syrup reaches 240°F (115°C), start to beat the second half of the egg whites to form stiff peaks.

03

Pour the sugar solution at 245°F (118°C) onto the beaten egg whites. Whisk and allow to cool to 120°F (50°C).

04

Work this meringue into the sugar almond mixture, and mix it all together, allowing it to settle. Pour it into a pastry bag fitted with a No. 11 nozzle.

**05**

Pipe circles of the paste, approximately 1½-inch (3.5-cm) in diameter, spacing them 1-inch (2-cm) apart on a tray lined with parchment paper or on a Silpat mat*. Tap the tray on the work surface, covered with a tea-towel.

**06**

Using a sieve, sprinkle the shells with a dusting of cocoa powder. Leave them to form a crust, for at least 30 minutes, at room temperature.

Preheat a convection oven to 350°F (180°C). Place the tray in the oven and bake for 12 minutes, opening and closing the oven door quickly twice during baking. Take them out of the oven, slide the shells onto the work surface and leave to cool.

07

Pour the ganache into a pastry bag fitted with a No. 11 nozzle. Pipe it generously on to half of the shells. Cover them with the other shells. Take them out of the refrigerator 2 hours before serving.

08

*Keep the macarons in the refrigerator for 24 hours, because they will be better the next day.*

# GLOSSARY

# GLOS-SARY

### BAIN-MARIE
A gentle way of cooking food, either in a double boiler or a bowl placed over a container of boiling water.

### CHINOIS
A conical strainer used to filter sauces or other preparations.

### COOKING CHOCOLATE
Chocolate that is very rich in cocoa butter, used in pâtisserie and confectionery.

### CRUST
Dry the shells of macarons before cooking so that their surface hardens slightly and no longer sticks when touched with a finger.

### EGG WHITES: OLD OR LIQUID
Egg whites, when a few days old, and stored at room temperature, are more liquid. They make better meringue, which doesn't collapse so easily.

### EMULSIFY
Beat a preparation vigorously, so as to incorporate air into the mixture.

### GANACHE
A preparation based on cream and chocolate (white, dark, or milk) that is used to decorate pastries or macarons.

### "GUITAR" PAPER
Thin sheets of transparent plastic that give chocolate a sheen. You can easily replace them with plastic sleeves used for filing, available at stationery stores.

### LINE
Cover the sides and base of a mold or ring with parchment paper, or with rolled-out pastry, pressing it lightly against the base and rim.

### MILLEFEUILLE
This literally means "a thousand leaves": Millefeuille is a pastry made of thin layers of puff pastry with layers of cream.

### PECTIN
Gelling substance naturally present in some fruits (apples, lemons).

### PIPE
Use a pastry bag to squeeze a mixture into a mold or tart.

### PISTACHIO PASTE
Chopped, crushed pistachios that give a green color to a mixture.

## S

### SEPARATION
Detachment of the molecules of fat from the rest of the preparation. To homogenize the preparation, whisk vigorously.

### SIFTING
Eliminates lumps and gives a fine, regular powder.

### SILPAT MATS
Silicone mats used for cooking or freezing. They can be bought in specialty stores and can be replaced by silicone mats of other brands.

## T

### TABLE/TEMPER CHOCOLATE
Bring the chocolate to predetermined temperatures (depending on the type of chocolate) so that the cocoa butter, cocoa, sugar, and milk powder can crystallize consistently. The aim is to obtain a smooth, fluid, and glossy texture.

### TITANIUM OXIDE
White pigment that helps to stabilize the coloring of ivory chocolate. Can be bought at a drugstore.

## W

### WHIP UNTIL LIGHT AND FLUFFY
Whip a preparation vigorously to lighten its consistency and increase its volume by incorporating as much air as possible.

# BASIC RECIPES

## ITALIAN MERINGUE

- ❏ ⅓ cup (75 ml) mineral water
- ❏ 8 ¾ oz (250 g) superfine sugar
- ❏ 4 egg whites (125 g/4 ½ oz)

Bring the water and sugar to a boil in a saucepan. As soon as the mixture boils, clean down the edges of the saucepan with a damp pastry brush. Leave to cook to 245°F (118°C). Beat the egg whites to soft peaks (that is, not too firm). Pour the sugar syrup onto the beaten egg whites. Allow to cool while continuing to beat.

## FRENCH MERINGUE

- ❏ 3 egg whites (3 ½ oz/100 g)
- ❏ 7 oz (200 g) superfine sugar

Put the egg whites into the bowl of a mixer fitted with the whisk; whip at medium speed, until they double in volume, incorporating 1½ oz (35 g) of sugar, and continue to whisk until they become very firm, very smooth, and very glossy, while adding another 2 oz (65 g) of sugar. Detach the mixer bowl and fold in 3 ½ oz (100 g) of sugar in a steady stream, lifting the meringue with a spatula, and working it as little as possible. Use immediately.

## ENGLISH CUSTARD

- ❏ 7 egg yolks (140 g/5 oz)
- ❏ 3 oz (80 g) superfine sugar
- ❏ 180 ml (¾ cup) fresh whole milk

Mix the yolks with the sugar. Bring the milk to a boil and pour it over the yolks and sugar. Whip and return to the pan before cooking it to 180°F (85°C). Run a finger along the back of a spatula coated with custard: it's ready if the track remains visible. Allow to cool and store in the refrigerator.

# DACQUOISE BISCUIT WITH HAZELNUTS

- ❐ 7 ½ oz (210 g) ground hazelnuts
- ❐ 8 oz (230 g) confectioners sugar
- ❐ 8 egg whites (8 oz/230 g)
- ❐ 3 oz (75 g) superfine sugar
- ❐ 2 ½ oz (70 g) roasted hazelnuts, crushed

On a baking sheet covered with parchment paper, roast the ground hazelnuts in the oven at 300°F (150°C) for 10 minutes. Sieve together the confectioners sugar and the roasted ground hazelnuts. Beat the egg whites, adding the superfine sugar in three batches, until you get a soft meringue. By hand, add the sieved mixture, gently lifting and turning the preparation with a spatula. Lay a baking frame on a tray covered with a sheet of parchment paper, and spread the preparation evenly using an angled offset spatula; sprinkle the crushed hazelnuts evenly over the top. Bake in a convection oven at 340°F (170°C) for approximately 30 minutes, quickly opening and closing the oven door once to prevent the dacquoise from rising and falling due to the concentration of steam in the oven.

# CHANTILLY

- ❐ ⅔ cup (150 ml) very cold whipping cream
- ❐ 1 teaspoon confectioners sugar

Beat the cream using a whisk or mixer. Starting at a low speed, increase the speed. Toward the end, add a level teaspoon of confectioners sugar.

# INVERTED PUFF PASTRY

- ❐ 13 ¼ oz (375 g) butter
- ❐ 1 lb 1 oz (500 g) T45 flour
- ❐ ⅔ cup (150 ml) mineral water
- ❐ ½ oz (17, 5 g) fleur de sel
- ❐ 4 oz (115 g) butter
- ❐ A few drops white vinegar

Work the butter and 5 ¼ oz (150 g) of flour together so that they are completely mixed. Form into a flattened ball and wrap in plastic before putting in the refrigerator for an hour. Relax the dough by mixing in the rest of the ingredients, form into a square, wrap in plastic, and allow to rest for an hour. Roll the pastry out into an oblong, fold the ends to the center, and then fold in two. This is the first double turn. Put back in the refrigerator for 2 hours and repeat the procedure. Return it in the refrigerator for another 2 hours and then give it a single turn: Roll out the pastry, fold in one-third and then fold the second third on top. Roll out the puff pastry, then cut it to shape and prick it with a fork. Place a sheet of parchment paper on the tray and lay the pastry on top. Place the tray in the refrigerator for at least 2 hours so that it rises well in the oven and cooks without shrinking. You can store the scraps in the freezer.

# BASIC RECIPES

## JOCONDE BISCUIT

- ❏ 1 oz (30 g) unsalted butter
- ❏ 5 ¼ oz (150 g) ground almonds
- ❏ 4 ¼ oz (120 g) confectioners sugar
- ❏ 4 whole eggs (7 oz/200 g)
- ❏ 4 egg whites (4 ¾ oz/130 g)
- ❏ 1 oz (20 g) superfine sugar
- ❏ 1½ oz (40 g) T55 flour

Melt the butter. Put the ground almonds and confectioners sugar into the bowl of a mixer fitted with the whisk, pour in half of the whole eggs, and beat for 8 minutes. Add the remaining whole eggs in two batches and beat for 10 to 12 minutes. Pour a little of this mixture into the melted butter and whisk. Beat the egg whites with the superfine sugar to stiff peaks, and pour it on the first preparation. Add the flour in a steady stream and stir gently before incorporating the butter into the mixture. Spread out the Joconde biscuit on a Silpat mat* or a piece of parchment paper, using an angled offset spatula. Bake in a convection oven at 450°F (230°C) for 5 minutes. Be careful not to brown the biscuit too much.

## CHOCOLATE SAUCE

- ❏ 4 ¾ oz (130 g) 70% cocoa Guanaja chocolate from Valrhona
- ❏ 1 cup (250 ml) water
- ❏ 3 ¼ oz (90 g) superfine sugar
- ❏ 4 ½ oz (125 g) heavy cream

Break the chocolate into pieces; put it in a large saucepan with the water, sugar, and cream. Bring to a boil over low heat; continue to boil over low heat, mixing with a spatula until the sauce coats the spatula and becomes as smooth as desired.

## CONFECTIONERS' CUSTARD

- ❏ 2 cups (580 ml) whole milk
- ❏ ½ oz (5 g) vanilla pods
- ❏ 1 tablespoon (15 g) flour
- ❏ 1 ½ oz (45 g) powdered milk
- ❏ 5 ¼ oz (150 g) superfine sugar
- ❏ 7 egg yolks (5 oz/140 g)
- ❏ 2 oz (60 g) butter

Boil 2 cups (500 ml) of the whole milk with the vanilla pods and leave to infuse for 20 minutes. Strain this infusion through a chinois*. Sieve the flour and powdered milk together. Add the vanilla infusion to one third of the superfine sugar and bring to a boil. Mix the egg yolks with the powdered milk and flour and the rest of the sugar. Add the remaining whole milk, a little at a time, mixing carefully. Bring the custard to a boil and cook for 5 minutes, stirring briskly with a whisk, then turn it into a bowl to cool. Add the butter at 120/85°F (50/30°C). Place the custard in an airtight container with a layer of plastic on the surface (to prevent a skin from forming) and store in the refrigerator.

# BUTTERCREAM

- ❏ ¾ cup (180 ml) fresh whole milk
- ❏ 5 oz (140 g) egg yolks
- ❏ 6 ½ oz (180 g) superfine sugar
- ❏ 1 lb 10 oz (750 g) unsalted butter, at room temperature
- ❏ 6 ¼ oz (175 g) Italian meringue

Heat the milk, egg yolks, and sugar together (like a custard) to 180°F (85°C), then cool in a mixer, at high speed. In the mixer, using the whisk, whip the butter until light and fluffy, add the custard and mix well. Detach the whisk and work in the Italian meringue by hand. Place in an airtight container and store in the refrigerator.

# CHIFFON CREAM

- ❏ 5 oz (140 g) confectioners' custard
- ❏ 1 lb 10 oz (745 g) buttercream
- ❏ scant ¾ cup (165 ml) whipping cream, whipped

In a bowl, soften the confectioners' custard with a whisk. In a mixer, whip the buttercream until it is light and fluffy*, then add the confectioners' custard. Detach the beaters and work in the whipped cream by hand. Use immediately.

# PIERRE HERMÉ'S ADDRESS BOOK

WWW.PIERREHERME.COM

## PARIS

4, RUE CAMBON, PARIS 1ER

39, AVENUE DE L'OPÉRA
PARIS 2e

18, RUE SAINTE CROIX DE
LA BRETONNERIE
PARIS 4e

72, RUE BONAPARTE
PARIS 6e

4 RUE CAMBON
PARIS 1ER

89, BOULEVARD
MALESHERBES
PARIS 8e

in the PUBLICIS DRUGSTORE
133, AVENUE DES CHAMPS
ÉLYSÉES
PARIS 8e

in GALERIES LAFAYETTE, in
the ESPACE SOULIERS and
ESPACE LUXE
40, BOULEVARD
HAUSSMANN
PARIS 9e

in GALERIES LAFAYETTE
GOURMET
35, BOULEVARD
HAUSSMANN
PARIS 9e

185, RUE DE VAUGIRARD
PARIS 15e

58, AVENUE PAUL
DOUMER
PARIS 16e

in PRINTEMPS PARLY 2
AVENUE CHARLES
DE GAULLE
78158 LE CHESNAY CEDEX

LA MAISON PIERRE HERMÉ
PARIS also prepares
desserts at the ROYAL
MONCEAU-RAFFLES PARIS
37, AVENUE HOCHE
PARIS 8e

## STRASBOURG

in GALERIES LAFAYETTE
33, RUE DU 22 NOVEMBRE
67000 STRASBOURG

## NICE

in GALERIES LAFAYETTE NICE
6, AVENUE JEAN MÉDECIN
06000 NICE

## LONDON

13 LOWNDES STREET,
BELGRAVIA, LONDON SW1

38 MONMOUTH STREET
WC2H 9EP LONDRES

in SELFRIDGES,
400 OXFORD STREET
LONDON W1A 1AB

## QATAR

LAGOONA MALL, WEST BAY
DOHA, QATAR

## AZERBAIJAN

PORT BAKU MALL
NEFTCHILAR AVENUE 151
GROUND FLOOR
AZ1010 BAKOU

39, AVENUE DE L'OPÉRA, PARIS 2ᵉ

# SOUTH KOREA

In CAFÉ DIOR
HOUSE OF DIOR - 5TH FLOOR
GANGNAM-GU
135517 SEOUL

HYUNDAI COEX DEPARTMENT STORE
B1F, 517 TEHERAN-RO, GANGNAM-GU
135-090 SEOUL

HYUNDAI DEPARTMENT STORE MAIN B1F
165 APGUJEONG-RO, GANGNAM-GU
135-724 SEOUL

# HONG-KONG

IFC MALL
SHOP 1019C, IFC MALL 8
FINANCE STREET
HONG KONG

HARBOUR CITY
SHOP 2410, LEVEL 2,
GATEWAY ARCADE
HARBOUR CITY, KOWLOON

in THE RITZ CARLTON
9/F, THE RITZ-CARLTON,
HONG KONG
INTERNATIONAL
COMMERCE CENTER
KOWLOON

# SAUDI ARABIA

ROSHANA MALL
TAHLIA STREET
JEDDAH

# TOKYO

THE NEW OTANI
4-1 KIOI-CHO
CHIYODA-KU
TOKYO 102-8578

SHIBUYA HIKARIE SHINQS
B2F, 2-21 SHIBUYA,
SHIBUYA-KU, TOKYO

LA PORTE AOYAMA 1F 2F –
5-51-8 JINGUMAE
SHIBUYA-KU
TOKYO 150-0001

ISETAN SHINJUKU
B1F3-14-1 SHINJUKU
SHINJUKU-KU
TOKYO 160-0022

NIHONBASHI MITSUKOSHI
B1F HONKAN 1-4-1
NIHONBASHI-
MUROMACHI
CHUO-KU
TOKYO 103-8001

# KOBE

DAIMARU KOBE
B1F, 40 AKASHI-CHO,
CHUO-KU, KOBE-SHI, HYOGO

# OSAKA

JR OSAKA MITSUKOSHI
ISETAN
B2F, 3-1-3 UMEDA
KITA-KU, OSAKA-SHI
OSAKA-FU 530 8558

# YOKOHAMA

SOGO YOKOHAMA B2F
2-18-1 TAKASHIMA
NISHI-KU, YOKOHAMA-SHI
KANAGAWA 220-8510

SHIBUYA SEIBU - UDAGAWA-
CHO 21-1, BAT A B1F
SHIBUYA-KU
TOKYO 150-8330

DAIMARU TOKYO NEW STORE
1F 1-9-1 MARUNOUCHI
CHIYODA-KU
TOKYO 100-6701

SEIBU IKEBUKURO
B1F, 1-28-1 MINAMI-
IKEBUKURO, TOSHIMA-KU
TOKYO 171-8569

FUTAKO TAMAGAWA
TOKYU FOODSHOW
BF1, 2-21-2 TAMAGAWA
SETAGAYA-KI
TOKYO 158-0094

MATSUYA GINZA
MATSUYA-GINZA FLOOR B1
GINZA 3-6-1, CHUO-KU,
TOKYO 104-8130

# DUBAÏ

GALERIES LAFAYETTE DUBAÏ
FRENCH DEPARTMENT
STORES LLC
CORNER PIERRE HERMÉ PARIS
GALERIES LAFAYETTE BLDG -
DUBAÏ MALL
BURJ DUBAÏ DISTRICT

MALL OF EMIRATES
AL BARSHA 1
GROUND FLOOR
118445 DUBAÏ

# THAILAND

THE EMQUARTIER
G FLOOR GB07
693, 695 SUKHUMVIT RD
KLONGTON NUA, WATTANA
10110 BANGKOK

# PRODUCT INDEX

PRODUCT INDEX

## A

ALMOND  18

ALMOND (FLAKED)  68

ALMOND (GROUND)  10, 44, 52, 60, 68, 78, 86, 94, 104

ALMOND PRALINE  28

## B

BLACK CURRANTS  60

BLACK CURRANT PURÉE  60

BLUEBERRIES  60

BUTTER  10, 18, 28, 36, 44, 52, 60, 68, 86, 94, 103, 104, 105

BUTTERCREAM  105

## C

CHOCOLATE  18, 28, 36, 44, 94, 104

CHOCOLATE – COOKINGE  36, 44

CHOCOLATE – WHITE  52

CLOVES  68

COCOA  28, 94

COLORING  78, 94

CONFECTIONERS' CUSTARD  18, 105

CORNFLOWER (PETALS)  60

CORNMEAL  44

CREAM  18, 28, 36, 52, 60, 78, 86, 103, 104, 105

CUSTARD  18, 105

## E

EGGS  10, 18, 28, 36, 44, 52, 60, 68, 78, 86, 94, 102, 103, 104, 105

## F

FLEUR DE SEL  18, 44, 52, 86, 103

FLOUR  18, 28, 44, 52, 60, 68, 86, 103, 104

## G

GAVOTTES  28, 36

GELATINE (LEAF)  52, 60, 68, 86

GLUCOSE  10

## H

HAZELNUTS  18, 36, 103

HAZELNUTS (GROUND)  36, 103

HAZELNUT (PASTE)  18, 28, 36

HAZELNUT PRALINE  18, 36

## L

LEMON (JUICE)  68, 78, 86

LYCHEE  10

## M

MAÏZENA  18

MASCARPONE  52, 60, 86

MERINGUE – ITALIAN  10, 18, 105

MILK  10, 18, 28, 60, 78, 102, 104, 105

MILK POWDER  78

## O

OLIVE – BLACK  86

OLIVE OIL  86

## P

PASSION FRUIT  68, 94

PECTINE NH FOR JAM  52

PISTACHIOS  78

POTATO STARCH 52

POWDERED MILK  104

PRALINE – ALMOND  28

PRALINE – HAZELNUT  18, 36

## R

RASPBERRIES  10, 44

RASPBERRY (PURÉE)  44

RED CURRANT (PURÉE)  60

RHUBARB  68

ROSE  10

RUM  52

## S

STRAWBERRIES  78

STRAWBERRY (PURÉE)  68, 86

SUGAR – CONFECTIONERS'  10, 18, 36, 44, 52, 60, 78, 86, 94, 103, 104

SUGAR – SUPERFINE  10, 18, 28, 36, 52, 60, 68, 78, 86, 94, 102, 103, 104, 105

## T

TITANIUM OXIDE (POWDER)  52

TOMATOES  86

TOMATO  86

## V

VANILLA  18, 44, 52, 60, 86, 104

VINEGAR – WHITE  18, 86, 103

VIOLET (FLAVORING)  60

## W

WATER  10, 18, 28, 52, 60, 78, 86, 102, 103, 104

**THANKS**

My sincere thanks to Mickaël Marsollier, Camille Moënne-Loccoz, and Delphine Baussan. Thanks to Alain Ducasse, as well as the Alain Ducasse Édition team

**DIRECTOR OF THE COLLECTION**
Alain Ducasse

**HEAD MANAGER**
Aurore Charoy

**EDITOR IN CHIEF**
Alice Gouget

**EDITORIAL ASSISTANT**
Claire Dupuy

**PHOTOGRAPHY**
La Food by Thomas Dhellemmes
www.lafood.fr

**STYLIST**
Chae Rin Vincent

**ART DIRECTOR**
Pierre Tachon

**GRAPHIC DESIGN**
Soins graphiques

**RECIPES PREPARED BY**
Mickaël Marsollier and Camille Moënne Loccoz

**PHOTO-ENGRAVING**
Nord Compo

**MARKETING AND COMMUNICATIONS MANAGER**
Camille Gonnet
camile.gonnet@alain-ducasse.com

*The editor warmly thanks M. Hermé, Delphine Baussan, Mickaël Marsollier, and Camille Moënne Loccoz, as well as all the book's creative team.*
*Thanks to Frédérick and Grasser Hermé.*

115 West 18th Street
New York, NY 10011
www.abramsbooks.com

Printed in China
ISBN 978-2-84123-738-8
Legal registration, 4th quarter 2015

© Alain Ducasse Edition 2015
Alain Ducasse Edition
2 rue Paul Vaillant Couturier
92530 Levallois Perret

# COOK
## WITH YOUR
## FAVORITE
# CHEFS